W9-ATT-244

The Beauty of
KOREA

Copyright © 1997
by Suh Jai–sik
Photo layout and editing also by Suh Jai–sik
All rights reserved

Published in 1997
by Hollym International Corp.
18 Donald Place, Elizabeth, New Jersey 07208 U.S.A.
Tel: (908) 353-1655   Fax: (908) 353-0255
http://www.hollym.com

Published simultaneously in Korea
by Hollym Corporation; Publishers
13-13 Kwanchol-dong, Chongno-gu, Seoul 110-111
Tel: (02) 735-7554   Fax: (02) 730-8192
http://www.hollym.co.kr

ISBN: 1-56591-074-5
Library of Congress Catalog Card Number: 97-74942

Printed in Korea

3 6645 00017094 4

CONTENTS

PREFACE

Korea is a beautiful country. The natural environment is beautiful and so are the people who work hard and make their lives here. The trace of our ancestors who made this land their home such a long time ago have not disappeared; the link remains strong as we their descendents continue to live on the same land today using one common language, finding pride and dignity in the continuation of our history and culture. Over the years there have been some very difficult times when our sovereign power was lost. But from such situations we have managed to rise up each time like a phoenix and reach the position that we have today as a free and democratic country. A small peninsula located at the end of Northeast Asia, Korea has many times been invaded by foreign powers coming over land and sea. But each time we have been victorious and now stand on an equal footing with other countries.

The purpose of this book is to show these features of Korea and Koreans. The book has been divided into seven chapters on Seoul, Kyongju and Puyo, Buddhism, Cheju Island, tradition and folk customs, nature and life and preparations for the 21st century. Knowledge of these seven areas is necessary in understanding Korea and its people. While the book is not one hundred percent perfect, I have put my heart and soul into it and present it with pride.

It would be gratifying to believe this book will give some insight and understanding into the nature of Korea and Koreans.

Changdok Palace is beautiful in all four seasons of the year but in the fall, the gardens come into their full splendor.

Befitting its name Snow Village, this tiny hamlet in the mountains receives three meters of snowfall every year.

SEOUL:
THE CAPITAL CITY OF KOREA

An aerial view of the World Trade Center in Kangnam where the
ASEM (Asia European Meeting) summit meeting will be held in the year
2000.

Seoul is a city that is always full of activity. With an area of 606.77km, one third the size of Cheju Island, Seoul is home to 10 million people which amounts to one quarter of the entire population. From a city that was planned more than 600 years ago, it has now taken its place in the world as an international metropolis.

Toward the end of the 14th century, King Taejo decided to move the capital from Kaekyoung to Hanyang, the former name of Seoul, in a bid to renew the spirits of the people. The location of Hanyang was an auspicious one in geomantic terms. With the Han River to the south and the Yellow Sea to the west, Hanyang had many natural advantages as far as transport went and was strategically placed right in the middle of the Korean peninsula.

Reduced to ashes in the Korean War, Seoul has risen up and been transformed greatly in the four decades since then. A population explosion has occurred giving rise to the saying that Seoul is a "full house." The growth in population has largely been caused by migration from rural areas. For more than 40 years political power has been centralized around the president and now, with the major financial institutions and conglomerate headquarters located in the capital, more than 60 percent of the whole country's resources are concentrated in Seoul. Not only that, but the nation's most prestigious universities are also all located in Seoul. For parents wishing to give their children the best education possible, this has been a motivating factor to move to Seoul. So in all respects, Seoul is the heart of the nation reaching out to the rest of the country through advanced transport and telecommunications systems.

What swells the population of Seoul even further is the vast number of people who travel to and fro from provincial areas and those who live in the surrounding cities of Kwachon, Songnam, Kwangmyong, Inchon, Anyang and Uijongbu but commute to the capital.

Big changes have also come in the physical appearance of Seoul. Just before liberation, the highest structure in the city was the five-story Hwashin building. But now within the original four gates there is a forest of skyscrapers and high rises. The slowly moving streetcars and rails of the past have gone and in their place is the subway system which has become an important means of mass transportation, with over 20 bridges across the Han River overground.

Traditional ways and customs have also declined due to the influx of Western culture. The construction of high rise apartments and the introduction of the concept of family planning has destroyed the extended family system while the rapid spread of christianity has contributed to the disappearance of traditional customs.

In spite of everything, Seoul manages to maintain a blend of the old and new. In the midst of the skyscrapers and busy traffic of downtown Seoul the great south gate, Soonglyemun, and the royal palaces of the Choson Dynasty can still be seen in their majesty, something that never fails to leave a strong impression foreign tourists. The Secret Garden especially is a place that retains, as the name suggests, a mysterious timeless beauty. These ancient palaces and gardens in the middle of the city are a great source of pride for the citizens of Seoul.

Seoul is in fact a popular tourist destination. Having been the capital of Korea for over 600 years, it contains many cultural relics and historic sites. Apart from the ancient palaces, there are as many as 109 cultural assets dotted around the city and despite being a busy metropolis, nature is not far away with the mountains and river in view. The view from the park on Mt. Nam in the middle of the city is spectacular and water sports can be enjoyed on the Han River.

Nowadays, Seoul functions as much more than just the capital city of Korea. It plays a major role on the world political stage and is the biggest city in the country bordering the last communist bastion on earth.

Through foreign invasions Seoul has been ruled by many different countries. Countless times the city has been left to ruin but each time it has risen up miraculously from the ashes, never losing its symbolic status in the hearts of the Korean people.

The important thing now is to take to heart the lessons of the past and make sure that we keep Seoul as the kind of city that can be handed on with pride to future generations.

Seoul is an energetic and beautiful place. The sight of the sun setting in glorious tones of red between the buildings of the city and the neverending stream of lights coming from the cars lined along the old city walls is surely a sight that is unique to this city.

Hosting the Olympics and various other international events has helped turn Seoul into a true international metropolis. The capital of Korea for over 600 years, Seoul is a big city, home to over 10 million people or 25 percent all South Koreans and the center of Korea's politics, economics, culture and education.

Reduced to ashes in the Korean War (1950-53), in the space of 40 years Seoul has risen up to become a prosperous modern city. It has grown at a dazzling pace and is now filled with skyscrapers and mammoth markets and shopping centers. In economic terms, Seoul accounts for 60 percent of the nation's wealth and is where the country's biggest conglomerates are headquartered. Korea's industrial structure is now dominated by white collar and service jobs.

Korea's economic revival has been called the "Miracle of
the Han River." The Han River which flows calmly through
the city of Seoul has become a place of rest and
recreation for the people who flock here on the weekends.
The river ferry ride has become a famous attraction. On
the riverside parks, holidaymakers play sports or just sit
and relax while anglers throw their lines into the water and
wait for a catch.

The Han River is much wider that other famous rivers such as the Seine of Paris, the Thames of London or the Rhine of Bonn. In measures 1.5km at its widest point and 50m at its narrowest. As calm as a huge lake, the Han flows peacefully through the backbone of the city of Seoul.

When summer comes, the Han River becomes a cool refuge for Seoul citizens. Water skiiers cut through the water, young couples ride pleasure craft and families splash around in the swimming pools set up in the riverside parks.

Seoul is not only the capital of Korea but also a city of international renown. The streets are alive with young people who in terms of style and sophistication are a match for their contemporaries anywhere else in the world. Apart from Myong-dong, long known as a little "Seoul inside Seoul," new centers of fashion such as Yong-dong and Apkujong-dong have congregate, is famous for its cheap but high quality goods and all tourists to Seoul stop here to shop.

The traditional extended family structure has broken down and given way to nuclear families. An outcome of this has been a rising trend for families to spend their weekends on outings together. The happy laughing faces of innocent children are a portrait of the future of Korea.

Seoul may be one of the most densely populated cities in the world but life here is far from being a dreary rat race. All manner of cultural events are held on the grounds of royal palaces and the city's gymnasiums and stadiums are filled with basketball and baseball fans. Seoul is a city where you can work hard and play hard.

Changdok-kung was the royal palace of Seoul for 300 years during the Choson Dynasty and it is particularly famous for the beauty of its garden known as the Secret Garden. It is hard to believe that such a beautiful secluded garden can still exist in the center of Seoul. Filled with pavilions, small buildings and ponds of various sizes, the Secret Garden embodies harmony between man and nature and is a breathtaking sight all year round.

Chongmyo is the royal shrine for Choson Dynasty kings and queens and it is here that the official state ancestral rites are held. Though it is located on one of the busiest thoroughfares in Seoul, Chongmyo is a world apart, filled with an air of gravity and peace. In December 1995, it was placed on Unesco's World Heritage List. In traditional Confucian society, when a king set up his kingdom, he first established a royal shrine and an altar to the guardian deities and then proceeded with the rites to thank the ancestors for their blessings and pray to the gods of heaven and earth to guard the welfare of the people. When King Taejo moved the capital of his kingdom to Seoul, he set up Chongmyo to the left of the royal palace and altar to the gods to the right. Chongmyo was destroyed in the Hideyoshi invasions in 1592 and rebuilt in 1608.

On the first Sunday of every May, the state memorial rites to the ancestors are held at Chongmyo under the auspices of the Chonju Yi clan. Chongmyo's inclusion on the World Heritage List was not due only to the value of its architectural structures but also the Confucian spirit which is embodied here. The roots of Korea's ancestral rites are in China, but in China only the buildings remain while in Korea the rites themselves have survived and evolved to become a unique religious ceremony complete with special costumes, processions and a music and dance performance called the chongmyo Cheryeak. The ancestral rites and the music and dance are protected as designated intangible cultural assets.

Within the original city walls built in 1396, the fifth year of King Taejo, Seoul is lit up at night like a sky full of stars.

A city that never sleeps, Seoul has survived through many foreign invasions, miraculously rising up like a phoenix each time.

KYONGJU, PUYO: HISTORIC CAPITALS OF THE ANCIENT KINGDOMS

Chomsongdae is a stone tower made in the Shilla dynasty that is believed to have been used as an astronomic observatory. The tower is made of 365 stones of a similar size piled on top of each other and one stone of around half the size. The number of stones equals the number of days in the lunar year.

When the spread of ironware led to the development of agriculture and military strength, the Three Kingdoms emerged and joined forces as one country. These Three Kingdoms were Koguryo, Paekche and Silla. Each kingdom has left behind traces of its own unique culture. Koguryo was located in the North in land that is no longer a part of Korea, but the cultural relics and historical sites of Silla can be found in Kyongju and those of Paekche in the city of Puyo. Kyongju is especially impressive. It was the capital of the Unified Silla Kingdom for 1,000 years and remains today as Korea's largest and most important cultural site and an internationally renowned tourist destination.

The history of Kyongju is the history of the Silla Kingdom which was first founded in 57 B.C. A wide valley surrounded by mountains and a stream running through the center, Kyongju had always been considered a good place to live. Tradition has it that the Silla Kingdom was formed when the six tribal clans who had settled in the Kyongju plains raised Pak Hyokkose to kingship.

Since its foundation, Kyongju was the only capital of the Silla Kingdom until it was annexed by the Koryo Dynasty in 992. In the meantime, Silla became the first kingdom to unite the various nation states into one country and in 527, the 14th year of King Pophung, Buddhism was officially adopted as the state religion leading to a flowering of Buddhist art and culture.

In 「Samguk Yusa」 (Memorabilia of the Three Kingdoms) Kyongju is described as having as "many temples are there are stars in the sky and pagodas stretching out in lines like a flock of wild geese in flight."

The first thing that most people notice as they enter Kyongju are the little rounded tombs that rise up here and there like small hills. These are the tombs of Silla royalty and aristocrats, the largest being 120m in diameter and 23m high. At the eastern end of Kyongju at the foot of Mt. Toham lies Pulkuksa Temple, one of the city's most famous attractions. Built 1,200 years ago during the reign of King Kyongdok, the name of the temple means "the world of Buddha built in the world of man."

In a stone cave at the top of Mt. Toham is another famous site, the Sokkuram Grotto. Mt. Toham was an important strategic military post for Silla and the Sokkuram cave temple was built there as a symbol of Buddha's protection of the nation. Sokkuram and Pulkuksa have all been included on the World Heritage List.

Forming the southern boundary of Kyongju is Mt. Nam, which is a huge historic site all on its own. Rising 494m above sea level, Mt. Nam is a place that bears witness to all the most important events of Silla, including the foundation of the nation and its demise at Posukjong. The mountain is a veritable outdoor museum filled with an abundance of Buddhist relics including some 100 temple sites, 80 Buddhist figures and 60 stone pagodas.

Every stone and blade of grass in the city of Kyongju forms a part of the city's rich 1,000-year history. Everywhere you go, everywhere you look is a precious thread in an ancient city that is no longer important only to Korea but to the whole world.

The first of the Three Kingdoms to see a full flowering of culture was the Paekche Kingdom. Many wonderful cultural relics have been left behind which suggest the splendor of the times.

Paekche was first established around the area of Kwangju, Kyonggi Province. But in 475, under Koguryo's southern expansion policy, the capital of the kingdom was moved to Woongjin, now known as Kongju in South Chungchong Province and once again to Sabi, present day Puyo, in 538. The Kongju and Puyo periods of Paekche were a time of prosperity and growth. Fortunately, many cultural relics from those times remain intact giving testimony to the richness of Paekche.

Like Kyongju, Puyo and Kongju also contain many royal tombs as large as 10m in diameter and 5m in height. Such tombs began to appear around the 4th and 5th centuries, built as a symbol of the power of the ruling classes as the authority of the royal court grew.

The tomb of King Muryong in Kongju was the first to be certified as a royal tomb of the Paekche Kingdom. Some 2,900 relics attesting to a rich and refined culture were discovered inside the tomb including gold earrings and a gold crown of national treasure level.

Kyongju, Puyo and Kongju—these historic capitals of the ancient kingdoms of Silla and Paekche are the birthplaces of Korea's brilliant culture. They are wonderful tourist sites which can show the world the spirit of the Korean people.

Built in 751, Sokkuram Grotto, a cave temple, was established by Kim Dae-song who also established Pulkuksa Temple. Sokkuram is a minature Buddhist temple built inside a mountain cave. In the center of the grotto, there is a statue of the Buddha sitting on a raised lotus pedestal. It is a Buddhist sanctum consisting of a main chamber and antechamber with statues of the Four Heavenly Kings flanking either side of the entrance hall. When you visit Kyongju, the recommended course is to visit Sokkuram first to cleanse the mind and spirit before proceeding to Pulkuksa. Both Sokkuram Grotto and Pulkuksa Temple are on the World Heritage List.

At the height of its power, it is said that endless lines of tile-roof houses could be seen on the streets of Kyongju. Today, there are many of those houses still surviving in the city. Located at the foot of Mt. Toham, Pulkuksa Temple is meant to be an expression of the world of Buddha in the world of man. The two beautiful stone pagodas in front of the main pavilion produce a wonderful harmony. Tabo Pagoda is fancy and carved in fine detail while Sokka Pagoda shows highly blanaced proportions.

Anapji royal resort pond is a place which attests to the splendor of the Silla Dynasty. Anapji was constructed in 674, straight after King Munmu unified the three kingdoms into Silla. In the one big pond there are three little islands and a mountain with 12 peaks which is a symbol of Taoist philosophy. The pavilions around the pond were the scene of great banquets held in honor of distingushed guests or on celebratory occasions.

Kyongju is known as a city which has temples as numerous as the stars and pagodas streching one after the other like a flock of wild geese. When King Munmu, who achieved unification of the three kingdoms, passed away he was buried into the East Sea where he turned into a dragon and continued his watch over the kingdom. The rock in the sea which is his tomb site is magnificent to see at sunrise.

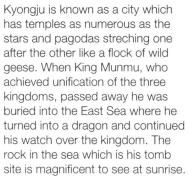

All around Kyongju you can see
numerous tombs swelling up from
the ground. These are the tombs of
the Silla Dynasty kings and
aristocrats. The biggest is 120m in
diameter and 23m in height.
Punwhangsa Pagoda is known as a
stone brick pagoda because it is
made of stones piled on top of each
other in the manner of bricks. Only
three stories are left today but it was
originally nine stories high.
Whangryongsa Temple, which is
beside Punwhangsa, once had the
highest wooden pagoda in the world
but it was destroyed in the 1238
Mongol invasion and now only the
empty site remains.

It is said that if one digs one foot under ground on Mt. Nam is Kyongju some treasure from the past will be unearthed. Each and every valley is steeped in legend and there are over 300 certified relic sites on this mountain which is a sacred ground of Silla culture. Yoon Kyung-ryol, known as a living Silla man, has discovered many relic sites on his own. The whole mountain is an historic site, attesting to all events such as the birth of the founder of the Kyongju Kim clan.

In contrast to china and porcelain, Silla ceramics were not glazed but fired in high temperatures up to 1,300 C. They were very hard as a result, not fine but rather earthy and massive in feel. Yu Hyo-ung has spent the last 30 years recreating Silla cermaic ware and has earned himself the title of "master artist." Silla ceramic ware from the 5th and 6th centuries are displayed in the Kyongju National Museum. The temperature and timing must be exact and only pine wood must be used for fuel.

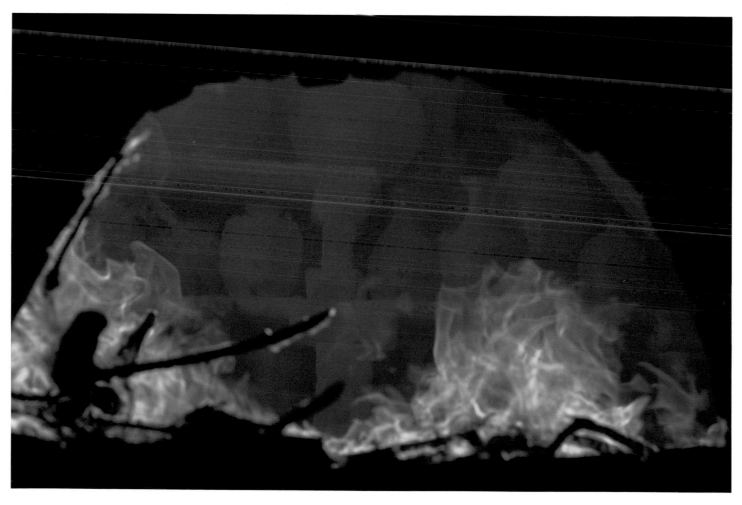

Silla Dynasty relics were first unearthed in Kyongju in the 1970s when a ten-year excavation project was put into action along with plans to construct tourist facilities and beautify historic sites. In Kyongju there are now 249 cultural treasures including 23 of national treasure status as well as 676 ancient tombs, including 38 tombs of kings. Excavation work continues today.

Founded in 18 B.C. the Paekche kingdom was the
first of the ancient three kingdoms of Korea to see
a great flowering of culture. In the different capitals
of the kingdom, there are many rich cultural relics
which attest to the revitalization of culture,
especially Kongju period (475-538) and Puyo
period (538-660) of Paekche. The mist gives an air
of mysteriousness to Paekche Pagoda which is a
classified national treasure.

The insence burner discovered in a Puyo tomb is an exquisite piece of artistry showing refined skils in casting and sculpture as well as expressing the life philosophy of the Paekche people. The Paekche people were also skilled in stonecraft. The stone pagodas and carvings which are the pride of Silla culture all had their roots in a Paekche culture. Like the Silla people, the Paekche people also made large tombs.In the tomb of King Muryong from Paekche some 2,900 relics have been discovered.

Renowned stone craftsmen, Paekche people left behind many sculptures and monuments and even the most insignificant brick or roof tile was treated with skill and artistry. But wealth and prosperity are always short lived. King Euija, the last king of Paekche, jumped into the Paekma River along with 3,000 princesses. Today a lone boat floats along the river which seems to wrap protectively around the rock from which the last tragedy of Peakche was played out.

CHEJU ISLAND:
TOURIST PARADISE
WITH EXOTIC SENTIMENT

Korea's biggest island, Cheju Island, is comparable in beauty to Hawaii or Bali. Cheju is a volcanic island located at the end of the Pan Pacific earthquake belt. It was formed from the outpouring of lava and 90 percent of the earth surface of the island is covered in basalt. Rising up in the center of the island is Mt. Halla, the highest mountain in Korea with a crater lake at its summit.

Surrounded by water and with a subtropical climate, the product of the island includes tangerines, pineapples and other tropical fruits. These factors also combine to make Cheju Korea's favorite holiday resort.

But the history of Cheju island is one marked by suffering. Covered in lava the ground is rough and the weather could be harsh bringing to the island a never ending series of disasters such as torrential rains, famine and epidemic diseases. In the past, the island was also a place of banishment for those exiled from court and a fort for the rest of the country's protection against Japanese pirates. The special products of Cheju, the ponies, tangerines and abalone, were paid in tribute taxes to the king.

More recently, the Korean War brought even greater hardship to Cheju as refugees flocked to the island. But these refugees also brought about many changes for the better. Among the refugees were many scholars, artists and writers who planted the seeds of art and literature in Cheju that had previously been a cultural wasteland.

From a land of suffering Cheju has now become a fourist paradise. It was in the 1960s that the island underwent development for tourism centering around Sogwipo. A road connecting Mt. Halla with the cities of Cheju and Sogwipo was widened and transportation improved with the regular arrival of passenger boats and planes. In the 1970s a plan to turn Cheju Island into an international tourist attraction was put into action.

With in the Chungmun resort there are many famous attractions such as Chonjeyon waterfall. Dolphin and penguin shows are held at the Royal Marine Park while the aquarium features all kinds of fish from all over the world. Yeomiji is a botanical garden which boasts the largest greenhouse in Asia containing 2,000 kinds of rare plants. Outside the greenhouse there are over 1,700 kinds of tress, flowers and plants that can be seen all year round. At Chungmun beach there are great sand dunes and room for horse riding and the site is often used for location shooting of films and TV dramas.

Leaving Chungmun, there stands a lone rock along the Sogwipo coast. This rock, known as Oedolgae, stands 20m high and was formed through volcanic activity that occurred 1.5 million years ago spewing lava and changing the shape of the island in general. It makes a magnificent scene with Bom island in the background.

To the south of the city of Cheju there is a cave dedicated to the three most common surnames of the people of the island where memorial rites are held to the ancestors every spring and autumn. Kwandok Pavilion stands by the road that goes through the city. It is a government office which attests to sovereign rule over the island in the past and inside the avilion can be seen an example of Prince Anpyong's writing.

Cheju has many waterfalls including Chongbang waterfall, a big waterfall to the east of Sogwipo which is 23m high and 8m wide and the only waterfall in the east to fall into the sea. The waterfall originates in the upper reaches of the Yong stream, therefore it continues to fall in the dry seasons and is one of the top ten sights of Cheju island.

Cheju is also home to the world's longest cave, the Manjang Cave which is 6,978m long and 7m high. Another of Cheju's top ten sights is the Sanbang cave temple, looking down from which the scene is majestic and beautiful.

Famous for three things—lots of wind, rocks and women—Cheju is the home of the famous women divers called "haenyo." The haenyo dive into the water to gather shellfish and seaweed without the help of any special equipment. They can stay under water at a depth of 20m for more than 2 minutes it need be. The haenyo are gradually disappearing from the life of Cheju island but they remain a solid symbol of the strength of Cheju women.

A natural environment that is a gift of God and a place of culture and history, Cheju is also now a world class tourist resort. But the real assets of the island are the pioneer spirit and common purpose of its people.

Often called a fantasy island or the Hawaii of the east, the island is even more attractive if you look beyond into the culture and history of Cheju.

From early spring, Cheju Island becomes a riot of bright rape flowers. Cheju Island is a volcanic island and Korea's biggest. Lying in the Pacific Ocean, southwest of the mainland, it is also the country's foremost tourist resort, famous for three things—lots of rocks, wind and women. Due to its natural beauty, the island has developed greatly since the 1960s.

Even in the middle of winter the temperature at the bottom of Mt. Halla, Korea's highest mountain at 1,958m, rarely drops below zero. But on the summit, heavy snow falls regularly and remains on the ground till late spring. The snowflakes and icicles are a different kind of attraction for mountain climbers. Separated from the mainland, not only the natural environment of Cheju Island is different from the rest of the country but the culture also. The haenyo, or women divers, are unique to Cheju as are the thatched roof houses surrounded by rock fences designed to keep the strong wind out.

The famous haenyo, or women divers, of Cheju search the sea for top shells, abalone, seaweed and kelp. With no particular equipment, these divers can go down as deep as 20m and stay under for over two minutes if need be. Their numbers have decreased over the years but the haenyo are still a lasting symbol of the strength of the women of Cheju.

The natives of Cheju, a flat land where all the lines seem to fall into the horizon, would look at the sea with sighs and tears. Though beautiful, the sea was a barrier to them and they looked upon it with despair. With a history of sadness Cheju Island was once a place of exile and its citizens were the subjects of contempt. It was also considered to be a fort against the invasions of Japanese pirates and the rare products of the island such as horses, mandarins and abalone were taken as tribute taxes to the king.

Horse breeding began on Cheju Island around 700 to 800 years ago and the Cheju pony was produced to suit the native terrain of the island. Designated a natural asset, the pony is smaller than most horses but very patient and strong. Cattle farming is still practised on the fields below Mt. Sanbang.

Legend has it that the nymphs came down to bathe at Chonjiyon Waterfall. Cheju has many beautiful waterfalls, including Chungbang Waterfall which drops down into the sea. An enduring symbol of Cheju Island are the stone grandfathers which stand at the entrance to any village to provide divine protection and drive away bad luck. There are still 45 original stone grandfathers on the island.

Cheju Island is full of sights not to be missed. The "lone rock" stands out in the sea off Sogwipo rising 20 meters high. It was formed 150 years ago when the lava from an eruption changed the shape of the island. To stand on this rock and fish for the snappers, which is a specialty of the island, is another attraction that only Cheju can offer. Because of its sub tropical weather and exotic atmosphere, Cheju Island has been called Fantasy Island and the Hawaii of the East.

Paekrokdam is the crater lake on top of Mt. Halla with a circumference of 2km. The water level rises and falls according to the seasons and the amount of rainfall but the lake never goes dry. Cheju Island was formed through volcanic activity. Most of the island is basalt and areas such as Mt. Sanbang and the islands Samdo and Udo are surrounded by rocks forming a bell shape.

Mt. Halla(1,950), the highest in South Korea, reveals the mystery of the nature and ecology. It has supported the Korean people as a mountain spirit.

KOREAN BUDDHISM
MELTED IN FOLK BELIEF

Buddhism in Korea is different to Buddhism in China or India. Buddhism came to Korea in the time of the Three Kingdoms, introduced from Manchuria through travellers coming over land and sea. Since then various factors such as geography, climate and the Korean ethnic traits have contributed to the development of a uniquely Korean form of Buddhism.

The first of the Three Kingdoms to embrace Buddhism was Koguryo. In 372, the king of Chin China sent a priest to Koguryo who presented King Sosurim with a Buddhist statue and sutras. King Sosurim then sent an envoy back to China with a letter of thanks and began to learn about Buddhism from the priest. Paekche adopted Buddhism 12 years later in 384.

In the Silla Kingdom, however, Buddhism was not so easily accepted due to the fierce opposition of the family clans who constituted the aristocracy. But the royalists who wanted to achieve a centralization of power rallied around King Pophung to suppress the opposition of the clans. They sought to make the law of the king the law of Buddha and the power of Buddha the power of the king. In 520, through the martyrdom of Lee Cha-don, Pophung finally succeeded in making Buddhism the state religion, thus providing an ideological underpinning for national unity.

It was in the Koryo Dynasty that Buddhism reached its height. King Taejo and his court had strong faith in Buddhism, believing that it was through the grace of Buddha that the kingdom had been created. Buddhism spread rapidly through Koryo and was adopted as the state religion.

In 1237, King Kojong began a 16-year project to create the Buddhist canon now known as the Tripitaka Koreana. Recognized as one of the most superb canons in the world, the Tripitaka Koreana is included on Unesco's World Heritage List. The 81,258 wooden blocks on which the canon is carved are now preserved at Haeinsa Temple, in Hapchon, South Kyongsang Province.

The period of Buddhist favor did not last into the Chosen Dynasty which systematically tried to drive Buddhism out. Priests and monks were forced to return to secular life and temples were taken over and turned into government offices. Under the oppression of confucian scholars, the Buddhists were took refuge in the mountains.

In each country Buddhism takes root, a unique faith and culture grows up around it. In Korea Buddhist art has been a very important part of the Buddhist culture since the time of the Three Kingdoms. The Buddhist influence was strong in architecture, especially stone building and pagoda construction. Many ancient stone pagodas still remain and attest to the skill and artistry of their creators.

When it comes to sculpture, it is Buddhist sculpture that stands out in our art history. Gilt bronze Buddha figures, stone Buddha's and rock cliff Buddha's from the Three Kingdoms period are among the finest examples of Buddhist art found anywhere in the world. The main Buddha found in Sokkuram Grotto with its peaceful attitude and mysterious smile is particularly revered and credited with arousing a feeling of deference in those who see it.

Buddhist painting is said to have flourished with the construction of temples, especially in the Koryo Dynasty. The most important Buddhist wall painting can be found Pusoksa Temple in Youngju. Painted in 1377, it is considered to be representative example of Koryo Buddhist painting.

Another important part of Buddhist art was handicraft, the most significant works being the temple bells and gongs. Silla temple bells were unique and the form developed during Silla was carried over into the Koryo Dynasty and a distinctive Korean type of bell was created. Generally rounded in shape, the bells were decorated with the figure of a writhing dragon at the top from which they were hung.

In terms of shape, sound and beauty of decoration, Silla temple bells are superior to those found in other Buddhist countries around the world. The bell of King Songdok (dated to 771, national treasure no. 29) in particular is a masterpiece of metalwork. large in size and fine in detail, shape and sound. The oldest Silla bell is that from Sangwonsa Temple (dated to 725, national treasure no. 36). This bell is said to have the most beautiful sound of all the ancient bells of Korea.

The influence Buddhism has had on Korea and its people is immeasurable, not just in terms of art but in terms of culture and society in general. Though Buddhism was once oppressed and its followers persecuted and driven into the mountains, the Buddhists have always come out fighting at the forefront of any national crisis and the culture that they have left behind is a source of great pride to the Korean people.

The Tripitaka Koreana at Haeinsa Temple which was designated World Heritage by Unesco is a Buddhist canon said to made with the help of Buddha of himself to protect the fatherland and save the nation. Carving of the canon on 80,000 wooden blocks began in 1236 and was completed in 1251. There are a total of 52,382,960 characters, every one of them beautifully executed and complete. Each year a special ceremony and procession is held to pass on the meaning of the Tripitaka Koreana to future generations.

Tongdosa Temple was built in 646
during the reign of Queen Sundok of
the Silla Kingdom. Considered to be
sacred ground, the temple contains
the bones and sarira of Sakayamuni
Buddha as well as the robes that he
always wore in his lifetime.
A ceremony is held in honor of
Sakayamuni each year on the
occasion of Buddha's birthday.

Buddhism had a great influence on the art history of Korea. The stome statues, gilded Buddha figures and rock cliff Buddhas still existing today reveal a wonderful technical refinement and mysterious beauty. The principal image of Buddha in Sokkuram grotto and other Buddhist statues there which are of national treasure status are not only works of art but objects of worship also. In Korea there are also many Buddha's carved into the face of rock cliffs. These images represent the merging of Buddhism and folk belief in the god of rocks.

The lantern parade which is held every year on the occasion of Buddha's birthday (eighth day of the fourth month of the lunar year) is a grand and beautiful spectacle. For Korean Buddhists, visting the temple is a year-round activity. At Unjusa Temple which is said to have been the site of 1,000 Buddhas and 1,000 pagodas, believers parade round the reclining Buddha to pray for the peace and safety of their families.

TRADITION AND FOLK CUSTOMS

Tradition refers to a basic culture that is handed down for generations. Folk customs are that part of a traditional culture that arises from the daily life of ordinary people from times immemorable. Thus folk customs have much in common with primitive and ancient cultures. At the same time, folk customs have survived through to the present day and still play a part in contemporary life.

The foundations of Korean culture from the new stone age and into the present have been found in agricultural society. Change and development came with the introduction and growth of Buddhism and Confucianism, leaving us with the folk customs that we know today.

Knowledge of the customs of the prehistoric age is naturally fragmentary and open to guesswork but records of the formation of tribal nation states can be found in some Chinese history books. In a book about the folk customs of Silla, it is recorded that "New Year's Day is a day for congratulating each other and preparing a feast. On the 15th of the eighth month, there is music and feasting." This gives us some insight into the customs that accompanied New Year in those times.

A look at the history of folk customs up to the time of the Three Kingdoms shows that the national games and ceremonies held at New Year and in May and October all had their origins in farming ceremonies and holiday customs. Such work as the weaving of hemp or silk also provided the basis for seasonal games and customs.

Customary rituals based on Buddhism first emerged in the Koryo Dynasty. One example is the lantern parade, a ceremony that is still performed on the eighth day of the fourth lunar month each year. Though the Koryo Dynasty was a time that saw the flourishing of Buddhist culture, this does not mean there were no customs related to Confucianism. A good example is the Festival of Confucius which is held in memory of the philosopher and spiritual leader. It is still performed today. The ceremony held at Sungkyunkwan in Seoul is particularly famous but it is also performed in many provincial schools.

Another custom that goes back to Confucius is the Korean people's worship of ancestors and it has become common to hold memorial rites on important holidays, at the tombs in October and at home on the anniversary of an ancestor's death. This shows just how large a part folk customs still play in our lives.

The decline of Buddhism in the Choson Dynasty made way for a rise in Confucianism and religious ceremonies emphasized the family ties of blood and patriarchy. The influence of this was felt not only in folk customs but has influenced life in general up to the present day as well as bringing about changes in the mind and spirit.

Towards the end of the Choson Dynasty there were many books and documents which officially recorded the country's folk customs, describing them clearly. It is these customs that have been handed down to us; they are our traditional culture and life.

The pattern of daily life took artistic expression in folk dramas which had their origins in farming ceremonies, funeral rites and primitive religious rites. Impromptu mask dramas, Puppet dramas and pansori all fall under the title of folk drama, as do farmers' music and riotous free–for–all celebrations. Shaman exorcisms were a form of art encompassing mask dance and often featuring a strong theme or storyline.

From a combination of folk customs and agricultural society there arose the genre of folk dance. The two main types of folk dance are religious dance and dance of the common people. Religious dances included those that shamans performed during exorcisms and those that Buddhist priests performed at the temples on special occasions. The dances of the ordinary people included artistic performances and large group dances which were closely related to each other. But there are differences in character. Group dances are usually productive, festive and unprofessional. They are more like games than anything else while artistic dances tend to be very professional.

Aside from the traces of traditional culture that have survived into modern times, there are many people who are the very carriers of tradition—the traditional craftsmen, dancers and musicians. To make sure Korea's traditional culture is passed on to posterity, the government has created a system of tangible and intangible cultural assets. It is these things that are unique to Korea and a source of pride for the people.

The flowing lines of the traditional hanbok and the rhythmic movements of the dancers at the height of the fan dance create the image of a flower in full bloom.

The folk customs of Korea are rooted in the traditional agrarian way of life and thus most customs arre related to farming work and seasonal celebrations. The representative folk music is farmer's music which is was performed to give strength and energy at times when the work got hard and to bring unity among the workers. Even today, farmers bands still exist in most rural villages and the riotous sounds of their music rings out on New Year, the Full Moon Day, Harvest Moon Festival and other occasions great and small.

The Bongsan Mask Dance, designated intangible cultural asset no. 17, begins with a street parade announcing the coming event. Divided into seven stages, the dance dates back to the late Koryo Dynasty and originated in the county of Bongsan, Hwanghae Province. It was a fete for the whole village performed on Tano Day, May 5.

Masked dance plays were performed by the common people who wished to ridicule and criticize the artistocrats through the safe anonymity of a mask. The performances would begin at dusk around a fire lit in the market place or in front of an aristocrat's home and continue till daybreak. Before the start of the play, a sacrifical rite was always held to ward off floods, disease and any other disasters. Afterwards, the masks were burnt and it was believed that all bad luck for the year disappeared with the smoke.

Traditional music can be divided into the two broad categories of court music and folk music. The major instruments used in Korean music are the piri(flute), kayagum (twelve-stringed zither), taegum(transverse bamboo flute) and komungo(harp). The music they create is not as elaborate of skillful as Western music but it has a peculiar charm and ability to touch the heartstrings.

The art of maedup, or knot tying, designated intangible cultural asset no. 22, is an art that has been passed on from hand to hand over the generations. There are 30 different kinds of maedup which has the characteristic of being formed in a vertical pattern only. Maedup is used not only as an ornament for clothes and interriors, but also musical instruments and palanquins.

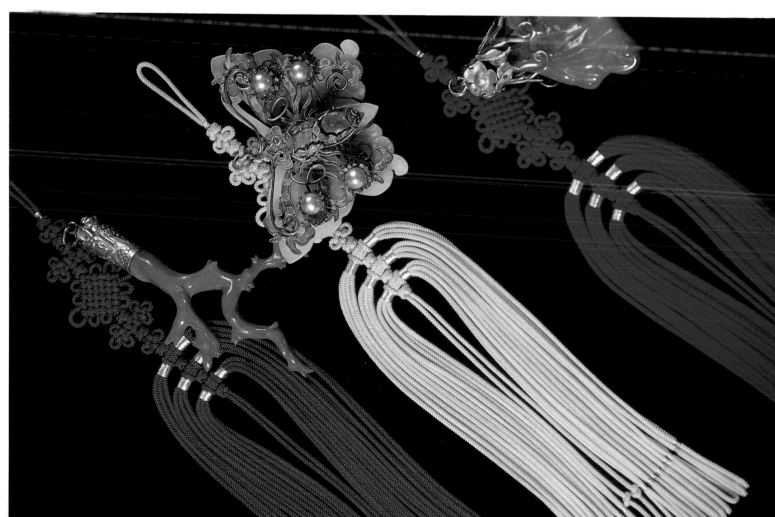

Patchwork cloths made with the humble scraps of fabric are a testament to the style and wisdom of Korean women of old. The patches of varying shape and size are sewn carefully together to create an item of elegant and softly shimmering beauty.

In Hadong county, South Kyongsang Province, there is a village which has been called the "porcelain Village" since olden times. Here potter Chang Kum-chong recreates a rough ceramic ware known as punchong that dates back 400 years.

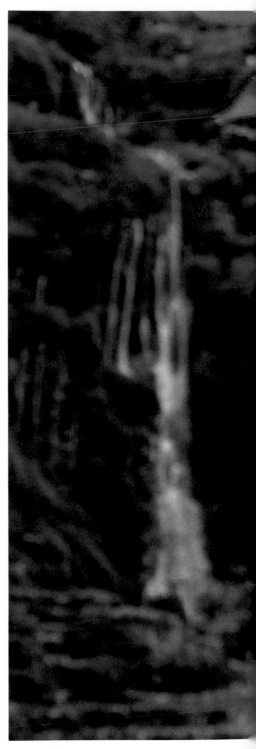

Maksabal, which liteally means rough bowls, were used by the common people of the Choson Dynasty. They were not refined and elegant like celadon or white porcelain but had a coarse beauty that seems to grow with familiarity. To recreate these earthy bowls, potter Chang Kum-chong says he has had to abandon all conventional skills and artistry.

Before an education system was implemented in Korea, the sodang or village schoolhouse was the center of all learning where children were taught Confucian ethics and the Chinese classics. Continuing the tradition at Namwon Sodang the Confucian teachings and traditional way of life are preserved with all students growing their hair long and wearing hanbok.

In the past, the common people often referred to the royal palace as the palace of nine folds, a name which indicated the mystery and solemnity of what went on inside the palace walls. Today, royalty no longer exists in Korea but the Office of Cultural Properties has organized reenactments of the grave and resplendent court rituals of the past based on references such as the "Annals of the Choson Dynasty" and the advice of scholars and experts.

From the period of the Three Kingdoms through to the Koryo Dynasty, the mainstream of Korean art was Buddhist art. The legacy is treasure trove of fine works including sculptures, wall paintings, temples and religious paintings. Many of these master works second to none in the world are preserved and protected as national treasures. In the Choson Dynasty painters such as An Kyon, Chong Son and Kim Hong-do began to devlop a native Korean style of painting which flourished in the 16th and 17th centuries. The artist who achieved greatness in the Korean style was Chong Son who took all the best elements of Korean and Chinese painting and introduced realism in landscape painting for the first time. Following him came Kim Hong-do and Shin Yun-bok who were masters of Choson Dynasty genre painting.

The Korean people boast of 5,000 years of history and traces of the brilliant culture of the past still remain. Many valuable relics have been and unearthed and are now preserved for posterity, while many more are still being discovered. These relics, which bear comparison with the world's finest, are the pride of the Korean people.

Therre are many ancient palaces in Seoul including the royal palace of the Choson Dynasty Kyongbok Palace, as well as Toksu Palace and Changdok Palace. One special feature of these palaces are their flower patterned walls, which represent the height in stone wall arrtistry. The wall around Chakyong Pavilion in Kyongbok Palace is particularly beautiful. Common patterns used to decorate stone walls include plant motifs such as pine trees, bamboo, orchids and crysanthemums, animals deemed to be lucky such as cranes and deer, as well as the symbols standing for longevity, wealth and status. The walls were originally built to protect the family and household animals but evolved to function as symbols of rank and authority.

Traditional sweets are made with loving care and look more like decorrations than food. Slices of dried fish garnished with crysanthemums, biscuits stamped with intricate designs, flowers made out of octopus and pine nuts—though they taste so good they seem too beautiful to eat.

Kimchi is the representative side dish of Korean food. It is estimated that Koreans have been making it from the time of the Three Kingdoms. The nutritional value of kimchi has been widely recognized and there are around 70 different regional types of kimchi across the country.

Korea is a small country but it has many mountains and rivers and four distinct seasons, thus making way for the development of a wide variety of foods. Food was prepared with a great deal of care and there were very strict rules for the setting of a table. Some dishes take a great deal of preparation such as "shinsolro" which contains 53 different ingredients and pressed meat slices made with trotters. Always ready to enjoy the good things in life, Koreans also enjoy their alcohol and each region has its own specialty that has been handed down over the years. Chonju is famous for its food. Chonju bibimbap, rice mixed with meat and vegetables, is particularly well known. The secret is in the freshness of the meat and the seasoning. Kabli and bulgogi are Korea's major meat dishes. To get the true taste of kalbi, the seasoned ribs should be cooked over coals.

For summer wear, hanbok made out of ramie cloth has always been considered by the Korean people to be the height of elegance and grace. Ramie is still expensive and it is Hansan ramie from Seochon county, South Chungchong Province that is considered to be the finest in the country. The traditional method of weaving ramie has been designated an intangible cultural asset and in Hansan the cultivation and production of ramie is handed down.

Quilted clothing worn in winter is made by placing cotton between two layers of fabric and stitching them down. In the old days when there were no sewing machines, the hardest of all the sewing work that was the women's lot was the making of quilted clothes.

The Korean people have their foundation in agricultural society so our folk games and customs are based on the seasons and focused on praying for plenty and giving thanks to the heavens. Out folk games date back to the time of the Three Kingdoms and were first

widely documented during the
Choson Dynasty.
The most detailed account is the
Hong Sung-mok's "Korean
Customs" from 1819. It records
details of games still existing today
including swinging, rope walking,
kite flying and making fire rings.

Marriage has always been considered one of the greatest responsibilities in life. This is why the etiquette and rules of a traditional wedding are so strict. At the wedding the ceremonial table must include lit candles, chestnuts, dates, persimmons, three kinds of fruit, pine leaves, bamboo, two vases decorated with red and blue thread and a pair of chickens which are meant to symbolize the legendary fidelity of geese. The groom faces east and the bride west as they make their bows to each other. Until this time the bride is not allowed to see the face of her husband to be.

A Confucian burial is regarded as the last honor of the Confucian follower at the close of his life. In the past when travel was difficult, the funeral was often delayed till after the last day of the month

of death to allow guests to be gathered at the event. An officiant went before the hearse driving out evil spirits while the pallbearers lead a long string of mourners.

What can compare to the mind of an aged mother as she prays for the wellbeing of her children? It is not important whether she prays to the mountain god, to Buddha or God in heaven but the spirit in which the prayer is offered. It is this spirit that binds all Koreans together.

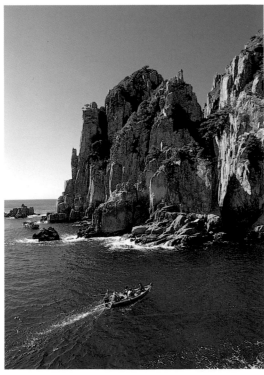

KOREA AND KOREANS, THE HARMONY OF NATURE AND LIFE

Located at the end of far eastern Asia, Korea is a small peninsular country where mountains, fields and seas create a harmonious landscape. The peninsula is approximately 1,020km long and 175km wide, and covers an area of about 220,000 sq. km. South Korea occupies about forty-five percent of the territory, or about 100,000 sq. km.

Located on the eastern side of the Asian continent between 33 and 43 degrees north latitude, the country has a temperate climate with four distinct seasons.

As a general rule, the eastern part of any continent experiences greater extremes in temperature than the western part as well as lower temperatures in winter. On the Korean peninsula there is also a sharp difference in temperatures between the northern and southern areas.

The weather is hot in summer throughout the peninsula but there is a sharp difference in winter temperatures between North and South Korea.

Precipitation is intensive in summer all over the peninsula with especially heavy rainfall in July in central areas including Seoul, and in August in the northern areas.

Farming, housing and transportation are directly affected by territorial features. Although Korea was developed as an agricultural society, the land is dominated by mountainous areas so there is a shortage of flat land for farming. But history has it that the Koreans settled on the peninsula to make their living here slashing and burning fields for cultivation.

With nearly 70 percent of its territory covered in mountains, Korea has long been known as a land of beautiful scenery. As the country has four distinct seasons and an overall temperate climate, each seasonal change creates its own unique mountain landscapes.

There are many great mountains in Korea, each with its own attractions. Mt. Chiri on a magnificent scale stretching over three provinces and five counties; Mt. Halla, the highest mountain in Korea, has a crater lake at the top; and Mt. Sorak offers extraordinary scenery with its rocks of fantastic shapes. Such mountains are popular for hiking and natural education.

Korea also has many limestone caves all over the Chungchong, Kyongsang and Kangwon provinces. Particularly in Taei-ri in Samchok County there are six famous caves including Kwanum Cave, which is considered the most beautiful cave in Korea. A natural cave located far from human habitation, Kwanum Cave is still in the process of growing and features various limestone formations, from the early stages of a cave development to stalactites and limestone pillars.

With heavily indented coasts in the west and south, Korea has a lot of islands. There are 3,200 small and big islands along the south coast alone and of them, about 500 are inhabited. There are also numerous islands of mysterious beauty.

In addition to the islands, Korea has a total of 20 national parks like Taean National Sea Park with its beautiful coastline and Hallyo Waterway National Park famous for its striking sea routes between small islands.

Ginseng is one of Korea's most famous specialty products, which has been recognized internationally for its medicinal effects. The ginseng root, which is shaped like a human body, has been treasured in Asia for thousands of years as a mysterious and miraculous medicine. The Chinese in particular have long prized Korean ginseng, calling it "Koryo ginseng." and recorded its medicinal effects in various literary documents.

Many people around the world have tried to cultivate ginseng in their own lands but so far, no success has been reported. Experts explain that the Koryo ginseng retains its original remedial properties only when it is grown in the Korean soil and climate.

Wild ginseng, however, has even better remedial properties than ordinary ginseng. Impossible to cultivate, wild ginseng grows deep in the mountains and it is said that only those with true and sincere hearts can recognize it. A single wild ginseng root can fetch up to hundreds of millions of won, depending on age and shape.

Living in a country surrounded by the sea on all sides but one, Koreans are actively engaged in the fishing industry. The East Sea, where cold and warm currents meet, constitutes a world–famous fishing ground and produces various sorts of fish, shellfish and seaweed. Each fishing village has its own public fish market featuring special marine products.

In all aspects, Korea seems to be blessed by nature. The Korean people have used their given natural environment with wisdom and diligence to build prosperous lives.

Located in the north of the Taebaek Mountains, the backbone of the Korean Peninsula, Mt. Sorak leads up to the Kaema Heights in North Korea through Mt. Kumkang and goes down south to the Charyong and Sobaek Mountains.
The highest peak in the Taebaek mountain range, magnificent Mt. Sorak is 1,708 meters high. It was formed out of a huge block of rock that was spilt and broken over time while its cracks became valleys connected in a ridgeline.

In this peaceful scene, fishermen gather clams in the mudflats while the tide is out. The west coast experiences a large difference in the tide's rise and fall under the influence of the country's unique topographical makeup where the eastern parts are high and the western parts low. The coastal mudflats, which shine bright in the reflected sun are a valuable source of living and a symbol of the abundance of the west coast area.

An ancient fortress stands proud as if showing off its flawless figure in an unpolluted environment where children grow up strong and healthly. From an early age these children learn through experience how to live in harmony with nature.

Agriculture is the
foundation of Korea's
development and is
still the basis for all
productive activities.
Now Korean farmers
are aggressively
improving the given
environmental
conditions by
reorganizing arable
lands and building

irrigation facilities and reservoirs. Mechandized farming methods and roads, which have opened up rural areas, have also contributed to transforming traditional agricultural villages whose residents no longer hanker after city life.

Although Korea's farming land and population have decreased sharply under the waves of industrialization and urbanization, agriculture still constitutes the firm basis of all Korean industries. These farmers, who have worked hard throughout the year and now are waiting for a big harvest, seem content as they sit down to enjoy a meal together. It is people like them who have created the nation.

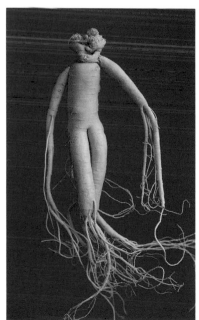

Already reconized internationally for its medicinal properties, Koryo Ginseng has been treasured in Asia for thousands of years as a mysterious and miraculous medicine. Koryo Ginseng cannot be cultivated in other country than Korea. The original remedial properties remain only when it's grown in its native soil and climate.

There are many Koreans who still hold onto the traditional lifestyle. Thet inherit the ways and manners of their ancestors and live them out in their daily lives. Maybe for this reason, their smiles seem to be full of serenity and peace.

A country, surrounded by the sea on all sides but one, Korea has an active fishing industry producing a wide variety of fish, shellfish and seaweed. Local specialties include the anchovies of the southern sea and the squid of the East Sea. Every fishing village has its own public fish market where fresh marine products are auctioned almost straight off the boat. A government plan to switch the focus of the fishing industry from catching fish to breeding them will first be put into action in Tongyang, an area known for its oysters and ascidians.

Traditional Korean houses seem much more comfortable and refined than houses in the Western style. Except for display models, most of these houses have disappeared but the descendents of some solid aristocratic families still insist in living in their ancient estates. With four distinct seasons, Koreans have developed various techniques to store foodstuffs against times they are not in season. "Toenjang" or soybean paste is still an integral part of Korea's culinary culture.

Covered with white snow, Kangwon Province makes a beautiful picture. Taei-ri in Samchok County, is a sort of hinterland, where traditional forms of houses like "nowa-jip" and "kulpi-jip" can be found. Nowa-jip have roofs made of thin oak tiles and a small window called "kogul" which serves as a lighting system.

It snows a lot in Kangwon Province. In places like Kosong and Pyongchang, where winter seems to last longer, the people live almost literally buried in snow. Under the snow, rice paddies, fields and roads all meld into and on some mornings people wake up to find their doors won't open as the house has been buried under snow overnight. Most of the residents here believe in a folk religion typical to mountainous areas, where they worship the shrines of trees of tutelary deities.

In a valley on a summer day, clean water falls like a blind on moss-grown rocks. Changing its colors according to the seasons, the natural landscape of Korea is beautiful. In back regions where visitors are rare, such beautiful. In back regions where visitors are rare, such beauty can be mystical. This natural environment cannot be called anything but a blessing from God.

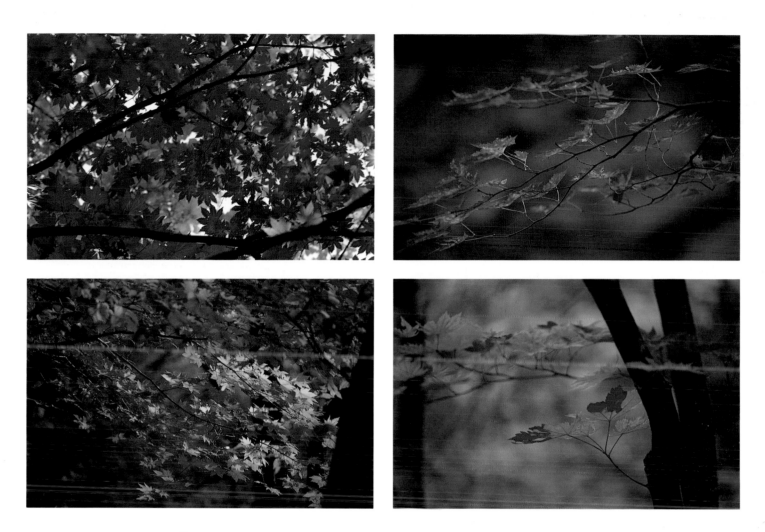

Clean water falls and branches off as it slides down the rocks of Murung Valley, which is resplendent in its autumn colors. The clear water catches the burnished red of the maple leaves and runs like liquid fire over the rock formations. As autumn comes the maple leaves turn from their summer green into red and gold and sway like flames in the wind.

Mt. Sorak can be divided into inner Sorak and outer Sorak. While outer Sorak is on a grand scale with high rocky peaks, inner Sorak is a paradise for climbers with its small peaks and fresh valleys. All the mountains in Korea, including Mt. Sorak, have a diversity of wild flowers which are different according to the seasons.

A sight of the clouded sea, seen from Chonhwang Peak in the national park of Mt. Wolchul (standing 808.7 meters above sea level). Cloud mountain ridges are unfurled as in a traditional ink painting. Mt. Wolchul has a lot of rough rocks and is hard to climb. Because of its fine scenery, it looks even higher than it really is.

Limestone caves can be found distributed all over Chungchong, Kyoungsang and Kangwon provinces. Particularly in Taei-ri in Samchok Country, there are six famous caves known as the Taei-ri Group.

They include Kwanum Cave, which is said to be the most beautiful in Korea, and the large Hwanson Cave. A natural cave in a place where people are few, Kwanum Cave is still in the process of forming so all the various stages of growth from the early appearance of a cave to the formation of stalactites and stone pillars can be seen in the one place.

Cheju Island is famous for its volcanic caves with more than 10km of them located close together in a narrow area, including the world's longest cave, Manjang Cave.

Hwaam Cave in Jongso, Kangwon Province, is a limestone cave which has been opened to the public and developed as a tourist attraction. The cave is made of a large single plaza of about 2,800 sq. meters, the largest of its kind in the nation. It has a primitive, natural beauty with its stone pillars, stone stalagmites, stalactites and stalactite walls. Geologists estimate the cave to be some 400 to 500 million years old and say that it is still in the process of growing.

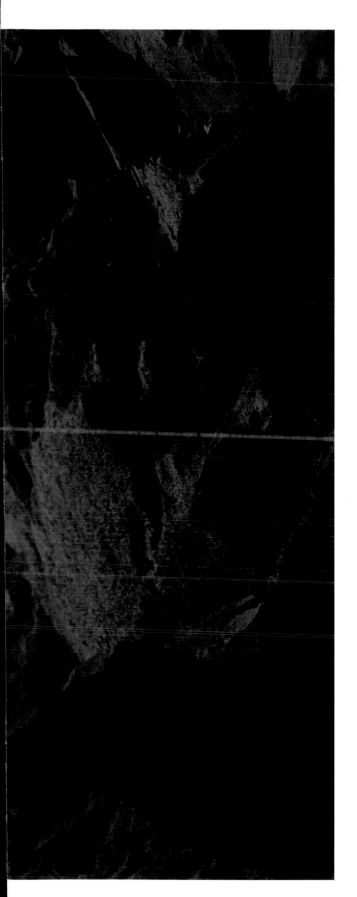

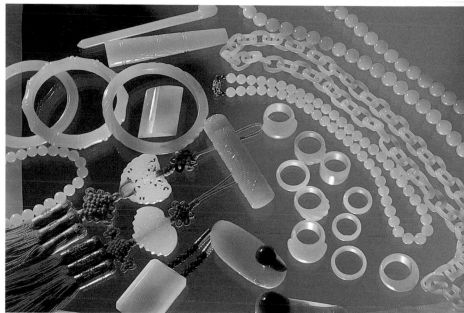

Jade is roughly divided into two kinds: hard and soft jades.
Hard jade is of a lower quality. Soft jade is prized as a high-quality gem and
has been found mostly in Korea and China. However, it is said that China has
recently exhausted its supply so jade can now be found only in Korea.
According to historic records, soft jade has long been treasured even before
the Three Kingdom Periods and was used for many ornaments such as
earrings and necklaces. Meanwhile, some say that jade is not valuable as a
jewel but also for its medicinal properties.

With an abundance of mountains, rivers and fields, Korea can be heaven for sports enthusiasts. On the weekends and in the holoday seasons, people take to the outdoors for a challenge with nature.

Surrounded by the sea, Korea has as many as 3,200 islands, 500 of which are inhabited. Hong Island, which was named such because the whole island turns red at sunset, is one of the most beautiful islands. Meanwhile, Korea is also a world-famous depository of dinosaur fossils. The marks of dinosaur feet have been found in such areas as Kosong, Kunui and Haenam, all in South Kyongsang Province. The world's largest dinosaur footprints have been found in Korea.

While the East Sea has a magnificent sunrise, the
Yellow Sea in the west is famous for its beautiful
sunset. The sight of a fisherman bringing his boat
alongside the pier at Komso Port, the
southernmost area of the Pyonsan Peninsula
national park, is the very picture of peace.
Surrounded by the sea, Korea features a rare
harmony of seas, rivers and mountains. It is a place
that has known relatively little of the disasters of
famine and war.

KOREA IN PREPARATION FOR THE 21ST CENTURY

An interior shot of Pohang iron and Steel Corporation (POSCO) which has been the driving force of Korea's economic development.
The company has a production capacity of about 21 million tons of crude steel a year.

After emerging victorious through numerous foreign invasions and national crises, Korea now stands as a free and democratic country on a par with developed nations in all aspects including politics, economy, culture and education. The Koreans have remained a single race throughout their 5,000–year history and outlived two devastating world wars in the 20th century.

Now Korea is preparing itself for the 21st century, in which it will emerge as an important player in Northeast Asia and a significant power on the international stage.

But In 1973 the country's first steel mill was completed and the world expressed its surprise at the feat. Since then facilities have been expanded with a fourth steel mill and iron foundry built in Kwangyang.

POSCO today now produces the largest amount of iron and steel in the world, marking an epoch in the history of iron and steel making.

The Koreans have worked hard with the belief that "nothing is impossible." Thus, Korea has become the 12th country in the world to pass the mark of $100 billion in exports and joined the group of developed countries.

An increasing number of local industries such as of semiconductors and shipping are world class. And the quality of life for people is getting better.

In the information and communications industry, which is expected to lead the 21st century, Korea is already on a par with developed countries. The government has decided to invest about 45 trillion won in the nation's largest project in history to build a high speed information and communications network by 2015.

The information fever has also spread to schools, many of which are building their own up–to–date academic information centers and multimedia educational support centers.

As far as education goes, an increasing number of schools are adopting an "open educational system," aimed at fostering creativity through conversations and debates held in a free atmosphere.

In the field of arts, Korea has already produced many world–renowned artists and musicians. And some of the country's most important cultural properties have been registered by Unesco on the World Heritage list.

Scheduled to be completed in 2020, Inchon International Airport is expected to be the world's best airport in terms of size and facilities. With an annual capacity to accommodate 530,000 flights and transport 100 million passengers and 7 million tons of cargo, the airport will become a hub of air transportation in Northeast Asia.

The construction of high–speed rail, a government project, will be completed by 2001. Estimated in 1993 to cost 10.7 trillion won, the rail is expected to bring great changes in the lives of Koreans.

Once opened, the Seoul–Pusan high–speed rail will be able to transport 500,000 passengers a day, about two and a half times more than the current railway system. It will drastically improve chronic traffic jams on the roads connecting Seoul and Pusan.

The freight carrying capacity on the Seoul–Pusan railroad will also be sharply increased to 3 million cotainers, about eight times more than at present. As the upcoming high–speed train will take only two hours to cover the distance from Seoul to Pusan, the country will become smaller so to speak. And thus, the functions of major provincial cities will be activated and the migration of people to metropolitan areas will be eased.

The national per capita income has already passed the $10,000 mark in 1996. As incomes increase, consumption patterns are also changing in a similar pattern to developed nations. People eat out more often and seek more leisure and entertainment. Accordingly, spending on transportation and communications has sharply increased. On the weekends, cars full of people can be seen heading for the mountains or the sea.

The demand for culture has also become very strong and many world–class performances take place in Korea while Korean artists are also actively advancing onto the international stage.

In 1996, Korea and Japan were selected as co–hosts of the 2002 World Cup soccer finals. This means that the world will turn its attention to Korea once again early in the 21st century.

In the north, Mt. Pukhan stands imposingly against the blue sky, like a symbol of the Korean people who are preparing themselves for the 21st century.

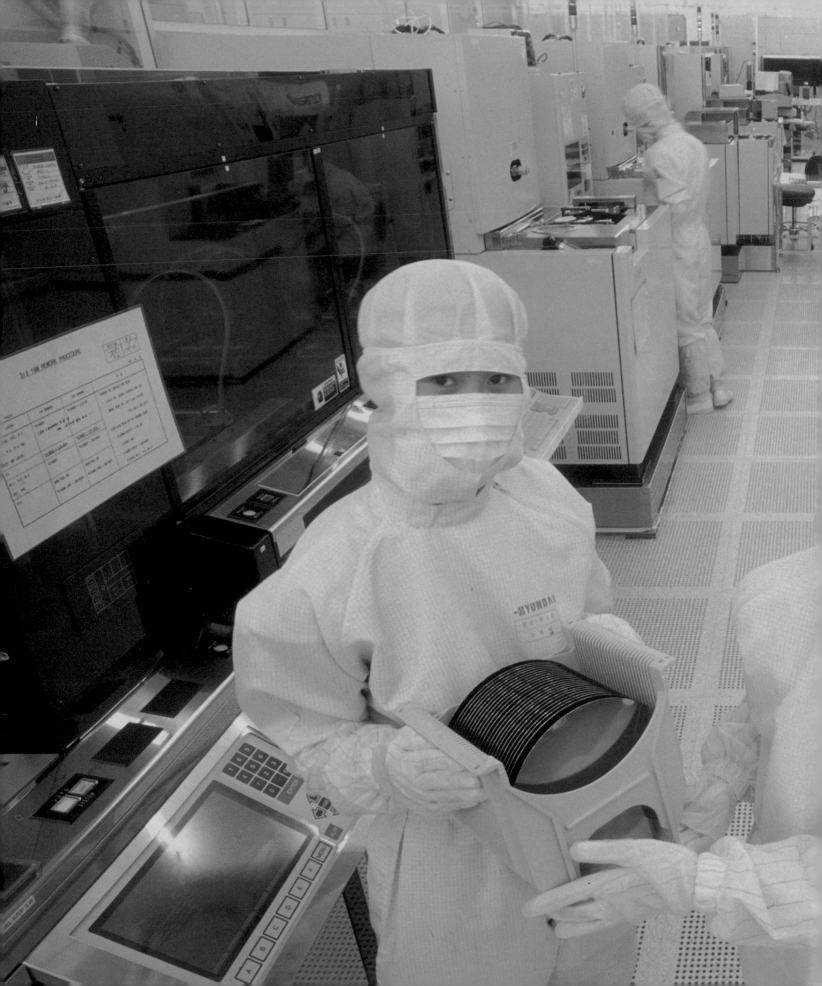

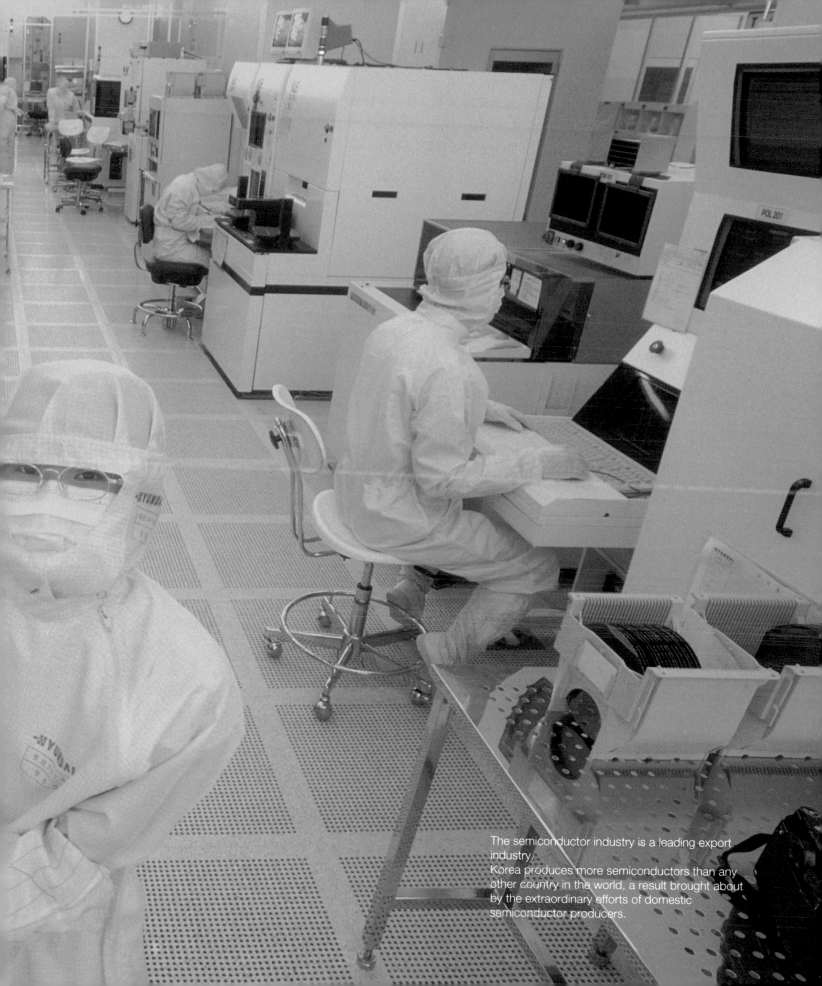

The semiconductor industry is a leading export industry.
Korea produces more semiconductors than any other country in the world, a result brought about by the extraordinary efforts of domestic semiconductor producers.

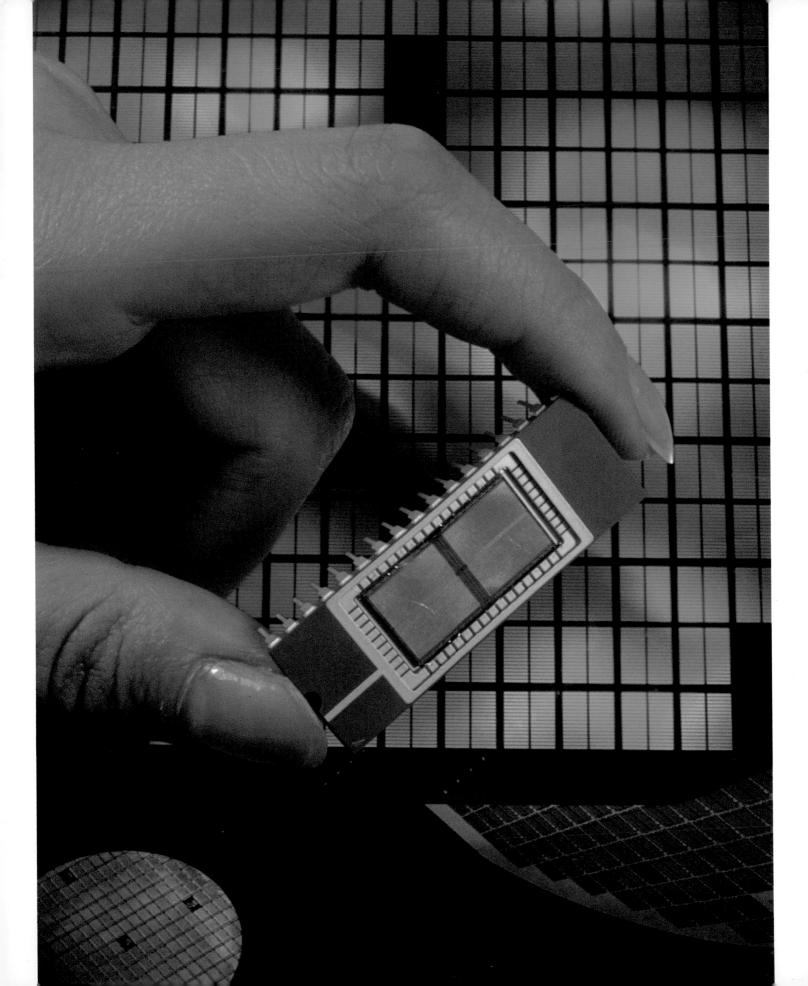

In the field of information and communications which will lead the 21st century, Korea is already on a par with developed countries.

The information fever has spread to academia and many schools are building their own information centers and multimedia educational support centers. The government has also decided to invest about 45 trillion won in creating a high-speed information and commu-nications network by 2015. It will be the largest public project in the country's history.

Along with semiconductors, another industry in which Korea leads the world is shipping. Korea has the skills to build high-technology ships such as double-structured ships and LNG carriers.

The lights keep burning far into the night in this industrial complex, displaying the inexhaustible diligence of Koreans. Despite numerous foreign invasions and national crises, the Korean people have worked hard wiht a can-do spirit and are now preparing to meet the 21st century.

The automobile industry is one Korea's leading export industries with an international competitveness earned through the installation of unmanned robotic manufacturing systems. In about 10 countried around the world, Korean cars take first place among all imported cars. The nation is also the 12th to have passed the mark of $10 million in annual automobile exports.

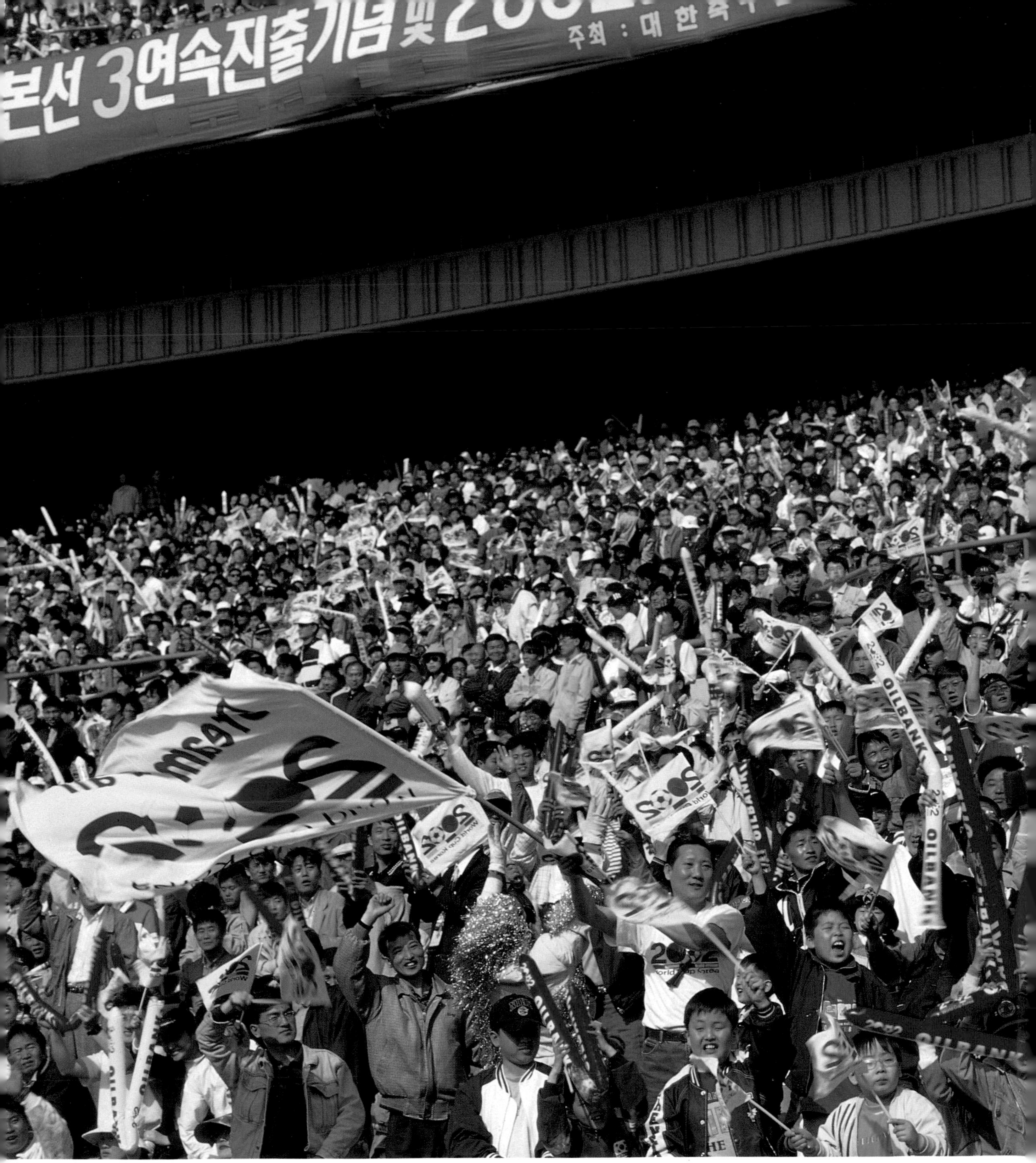
본선 3연속진출기념 및
주최 : 대 한 축
OILBANK
2002
World Cup Korea

The first big soccer festival of the 21st century, the 2002 World Cup will be jointly hosted by Korea and Japan. So far, 11 nations have hosted the World Cup and of them, only seven have hosted the Olympics as well. That Korea is one of those seven countries proves its international status. As a small peninsular country, located at the end of northeastern Asia, Korea has surmounted strong foreign powers from across the ocean, and now stands on a par with many developed nations.

Cover: Traditional Korean style quilted dresses
are favored by many women today for their
classical Oriental flavor.
Kim Sook-jin often incorporates modern fashion
motifs in cutting and decorating her quilted
dresses.